A Quill with Nectar Drop

FanatiXx Publication
ISO 9001:2015 CERTIFIED

FanatiXx Publication
AM/56, Basanti Colony, Rourkela 769012, Odisha
ISO 9001:2015 CERTIFIED
Website: *www.fanatixx.in*

"A Quill with Nectar Drop"
By: Theva Kiruba
ISBN: 978-93-5452-267-3
Collection of English Poems and Quotes 1st Edition
Cover Design: Sagar Samal

Typeset by: BooksClub.in

DISCLAIMER

This is a work of fiction. Names, characters, places, and incidents are either the product of author's imagination or have been used illustratively and any resemblance to any person, living or dead, events or locales is entirely coincidental.

Efforts have been made to keep the entire content plagiarism free, in any case if a plagiarism is found, only the author is deemed to be responsible.

Theva Kiruba asserts all rights to be identified as the author of this work.

About the Author

Theva Kiruba, is a young budding writer. She has obtained English Literature from Holy Cross College, Trichy. She is very fervent to spend her time in writing. In her perspective, "Writing is a magic and writer is magician", they can drive readers to the new world. She is renowned for "TWIST" and that is her specialty. Always, she prefers Fantasy, love, adventure and Thriller. She especially loves Writing Poem, Reading Books, Doing Podcast, Painting, Playing Handball, Singing and hearing music. So far, she has been published three poems in an anthology from **"Spectrum of Thoughts"**.

"Memories of you" and **"All because of you"** in *Love Human and Hate Human.*
And **"Adam's Bolt"** in *Constellation of souls.*

You can listen to her podcast on following platforms under the name **Theva Podcast**

- **Apple Podcasts**
- **Breaker**
- **YouTube**
- **Spotify**
- **Castbox**
- **Google Podcasts**
- **Overcast**
- **PocketCasts**
- **RadioPublic**
- **TuneIn**

Acknowledgement

Thank you, god, for being faithful when I was faithless, for your unconditional love, for your guidance and every miracle that made this book possible.

I'd like to thank my parents, Dr. Catherin Edward, Dr. Sr. Judy Gomez, Devi shree, Preceleya and all my friends and Brothers and sisters for all their guidance and assistance.

Heartfelt thanks to Ishika Bhardwaj and of course the incredible Saizal Gupta, Sagar Samal and team for editing my book. Special thanks to Spectrum of thoughts and FanatiXx Publication.

GLORY TO GOD

THE TWIST BLASTING POETRY

Preface

It has taken a long time to finish this book. My heart dealt with countless emotions while writing this book. And it reveals an emotional outburst.

I have treasured all my thoughts and have given them safely into your hands. Take care of them all safely.

Contents

THE DEEPEST BOND

A Beautiful bud schleps me so far;

This is a juncture for my florescence;

Your celestial honey alleviates my hunger;

My wounds are melting with your gentle kiss;

Your petal-like hand adores me;

We both are having deepest bond;

Yes, the deepest bond;

You are my beloved soul;

Your love sprinkle on me;

Your fragrance of breath sooths all my pain;

Your warmth cures my entire affliction;

I need one more time to sleep in your floret,

Yup! The Aesthetic floret,

To escalate, our Umbilical cord relationship.

A PATH TO THE HUGE WORLD

A Miniature Butterfly awakes me this morning,

That steers me through the attenuated path;

My eyeballs are rolling;

My effervescent vital force recklessly follows that butterfly;

Gentle breeze pinches my skin,

And apply blush to my cheeks;

Birds are legendary symphonist;

Their twinkling music gives me wings,

Oh, I'm flying!

Bees are treasure keeper,

Fairy queen is conceiving a table for me;

Queen bee serves me mysterious potion;

Oh, I stagger!

Sudden sparkling blast here and there;

Thunder plays its drums,

Wind blows the flute,

Cloud gives me a way,

An immense light hug me tightly,

In the long run, I perceive my soul in the hands of the god…

MY EVERLASTING LOVE

My Every Heartbeat says,

You are my sconce,

You fabricate me to gleam throughout my life;

You are my Falcon,

You steer me to dream high;

You are my root,

You help me to grow enormous;

You are my shell,

You furnish me sturdy auspices;

You are my breath,

Without you I'm nothing;

You are my everything,

My everlasting love!

You celebrate an ecstatic party for me;

At the end you honor me with crown;

You are my king;

And, I'm your little Princess!

THE CASE UNDER MR. CHIEF JUSTICE

There is a massive conversation betwixt the RBC and WBC;

That conversation turns into squabble,

Argument comes under chief justice:

MR.RED HEART;

Defense Lawyer: MRS.VEIN,

Emerge the case;

Lord, my petitioner RBC is nothing without him;

Justice probes, who is he?

RBC says,

Ice will melt before his love;

The Earth gyrates in backward direction,

Before his care;

The Sun rises in the west,

By admiring his affection;

Waterfalls freeze,

By wondering about his guidance;

Clouds disappear,

By sighting his tender heart;

Without him I'm nothing;

The chief justice astonishes,

They are arguing about the perpetual love;

Then,

Public Prosecutor: MR. BONES,

Says,

Lord, my petitioner WBC doesn't want him;

Chief Justice: MR.RED HEART,

Concludes,

He is a manufacture of our entire world,

Without him we are nothing,

He is non-other than,

Our Almighty God!

DAWN TO DUSK

It is a pleasing dawn;

The Sun shaking its hand with sky;

Cold breeze playing Hide and Seek;

Buds are blooming,

Ah!

Drizzling of snow gently sprinkles its droplet over the

flowers;

Symphonic pageant all over the sky;

Oh! It's echoing!

Yeah! Birds are my morning alarm,

Anna step - out from her house;

Chill breeze knocks her heart with gentle kiss;

Voice of breeze not able to enter into her heart,

Because Edward living there;

Now, they are in the exquisite ceremony;

Silver splash here and there,

Oh! That is coming from Photographers,

Giggling sound crossing here and there,

Yeah! That's from Anna's friends;

Fragrance of flowers floating in the air;

Red carpet is welcoming them;

Rings are waiting for them in the hands of priest;

Anna & Edward sharing their vows;

Anna blushes by the sight of Edward;

They are exchanging their rings;

With joy,

With love,

With purity of God's blessings;

Doves are flying away by hearing the sound of DING-

DONG;

Yup, that's the church bell!

Everyone rejoices in Edward – Anna's wedding day;

Anna! Anna!

Mother calling her;

Oh! It's my day dream;

Anna's lips get elaborate and her teeth shining before mirror;

It is a time to dusk;

Anna, preparing herself for another dream.

WHERE I'M

Where I'm,

My heart fascinates,

Your cold touch gives me warmth;

Your gentle breeze hugs my heart;

Your breath evaporates my soul;

Your beauty drives me to the heaven;

Your dazzling beats hypnotize me;

Your beautiful height mesmerizes me;

Your final touch wakes me;

Oh! My God!

My moments are priceless because of him;

Yes, he is the reason,

My falls…Huge Water - falls…

THIS IS MY WISH

This is my wish…

Yeah! Darling!

Holding your hands and walking with you for long distance;

You're my artist;

I'm your portrait;

World is a white paper;

Your first stroke is my shadow;

Your second stroke paints me with silver;

I'm glowing like an Angel!

Ah! You honor me with garland,

That twinkling stars;

I admire at you, my sweet heart;

Glitters just floating in my dress;

Spending my time with you is something special;

We often dance in the parties;

Stars are my huge music band;

They compose music for us;

I can spend all my nights with you;

This is a time to say good bye to you,

Because you are my long-distance relationship;

Yeah! My Moon;

My Moon, darling!

THE TARGET

This is the last minute of my life;

I start counting my breath,

My Heartbeat is yelling;

Lub-tub…Lub-tub…

Silence all around;

Heart beats a lot;

My body shivers;

Blood circulates in unusual order;

My mind rewinds the happening;

One hour before;

Thief enters into my house;

He sets his gun at me;

He presses the trigger;

The bullet shoots out;

It glares at me;

Whole world pauses for a second;

The bullet hits my body;

It tears into my flesh;

My heart is the last station;

Now, my mind wants to fast forward;

My eye starts to blink;

Everything becomes dark;

My soul wants to say good bye to my body;

My Alarm rings;

Oh! This is my dream;

That thief is my husband,

Thank god!

I'm alive now.

MY FAIRY QUEEN

Bella plays with her hair;

Sun beam showing his teeth;

Its ray passes through window,

And coloring her hair;

Ah! Her hair shining;

Then, the ray blushes her cheeks with gold;

She, shy's!

She dresses-up in white,

Ray glows her with gold;

Cloud honors her with crown;

Wind beautifies her with wings;

Her crown looks like nimbus;

Her skin is so soft like petals;

She spreads her fragrance everywhere;

She smells like Jasmine;

Her apple like cheeks,

Glaring the world;

Nectar floats in her lips;

Bees longing,

Coz, nectar from her lips sweeter than all flowers;

Her eyes look like crystal ball;

Ah! That is my fortune teller;

Robert smiles;

Because, Bella his dream girl.

I WANNA UNDIGITALIZE WORLD

Buds are blooming everywhere;

Birds creeping all over the village;

Bumble bee searching for honey;

Tuscan sun pushes back the clouds,

And shine like glitter ball;

Blackly shadow wipes everywhere,

And sun paste golden glitter instead;

The admiral river brings wealth to that village;

And that chill water wipes thirst of the villagers;

The entire village twinkles with golden-green;

Juniper trees spread breezy fragrance everywhere;

The cock beat the alarm;

Everyone wakes up before the alarm;

Corns in the corn field,

Dancing with the wind;

Butterflies kissing the flowers;

Villagers working in the greenly growing field;

Trees are best companion for children;

Children sharing their smile with each other;

They are the angels in that village;

Aroma of cooking coming from every house;

Yummy! To taste the grindstone food;

Mother's preparation,

Yeah!

It holds love and care;

Food distributing in banana leaf;

It is even healthier too;

Entire family members gathering together for lunch,

In the heavenly house;

Han!

Hundred year-old aesthetic houses,

Entirely adorn with floral designs;

Stunning lanterns here and there;

Admirable!

I think, readers you are in heaven;

Yup!

Now, your feeling lives in the Undigitalize world.

HORROR NIGHT IN MY LIFE

It is a dark night;

Stars hiding themselves behind the clouds;

Bats are the only birds in the sky;

Owl's sound echoing everywhere,

Moon shows the way to Mary, to reach her house;

Mary is shivering like a baby bird;

Her heart beating like thunder blast,

That looks like lighting splash here and there in the street;

She reaches her house;

She gets shock by seeing her house door already open;

There is no current;

The blood floats in the entrance door;

She looks pale;

Without making noise,

She slowly enters into the house;

She can hear clock sound;

Tic - Tic - Tic;

Each moves of the clock,

Raise her heart beat;

Her heart makes more noise than a clock;

She starts sweating;

A salty drop slowly gets down from her hand and reaches the
ground;
She driving herself to the bedroom through the stains;
She sensing that somebody following behind her;
The clock strikes fast;
Her heart is the best competitor to the clock;
She reaches her bedroom;
She slowly opens the door;
Suddenly, she becomes blind;
She is yelling;
I'm not able to see anything;
God help me!
She swallows saliva through her throat;
A stranger tie her eyes;
The entire world lost its strength;
The world moves slowly;
That stranger drives her to the hall;
He slowly removes that cloth from her eyes;
Sudden, outburst of joy;
Everyone sings "HAPPY BIRTHDAY" to Mary;
Popper blast,
Party starts;

Her mind voice loading,

Ah! What a horrible birthday party, I've ever seen in my life….

YOU ARE THE REASON

Someone is knocking my door;

I remove my quilt and get down from my bed;

My toes try to get into my sandals;

Clock strikes into 12:00;

The clock echoing into my entire bedroom;

Ding-Dong! Ding-Dong!

Silence paves the way to my each footstep;

Knocking sound rises;

Tok-Tok…

My hand starts shivering;

Slowly I open the door;

Two cops standing in front of my house;

They say you are under arrest in the case of murder;

They put the handcuffs around my wrists;

Silencer sound of the vehicle echoing into my street;

And the light of the vehicle splashing upon my entire house;

They make me to kneel down in the drawing room;

Both cops target their gun towards me;

They rolled their gun with bullets;

And press the trigger;

The bullet strikes out from the gun,

And hit my head;

My eyes stuck for a while;

My body slowly reaches the ground;

Blood slowly comes out from my head,

And floats in the ground;

Suddenly, lights on;

Applause sound echoing entire house;

Director says,

Well done! Good acting!

Yeah!

This is a "SHOOTING SPOT".

INTO THE DEEP FOREST

Long road drives me into the deep forest;

Breezy air purifies my soul;

Sunny ray playing hide and seek with me;

Bunnies are my little companion in the forest

I see that,

Birds taste the heavenly fruits;

Squirrels rolling their nuts into the tree holes;

Spider knitting the web in the corner of the tree;

Flowers spreading their aesthetic fragrance,

That fragrance, paves the way to the bees to find the flowers;

Nectar from the flowers is a heavenly drug to the bees;

They stagger and making sound like,

Wiz…. Wiz….

Sudden sound of door bell,

Ding-Ding! Ding-Dong!

Daisy's pen strikes with "THEY STAGGER";

She opens the door;

Her writing comes into reality;

"LONG ROAD DRIVES HER INTO THE DEEP FOREST"

THE DAMSEL WITH BLACK PRINCE

Pleasing dawn breaking in the morning;

My legs are walking through the blank road;

The roadside adores with floral bed;

Fog covers Entire Street;

Snow droplet from the leaf slowly touches the ground;

I can see that,

A horse standing near the bridge;

Royal black;

Snow drops are gently growing;

I get near to the black horse;

It gives me a ride to the new world;

Yup!

Fantasy world;

Horse enters into the magic hole;

Sudden shot of change;

Black horse into angel like prince;

And myself into pearl white princess;

Fairies are receptionist; they welcoming us;

I'm unable to believe with my own eyes;

This world is completely different;

Dwarfs are worker in this world;

Dragon is an another medium to travel in this world;

Mouse is a messenger; they passing message to me;

"Message from Dwarfs, they welcoming us to the castle",

Cats are doorkeeper to the castle; they standing near the gate;

Trees are two times taller than usual world;

I wonder;

All animals can speak in this world;

Elephant are chef master; they cooking tasty food;

Monkeys are servers; they serving delicious food;

Every animal calling me as a princess;

We just enter into the castle;

Dwarfs make us to sit in the Prince and Princess chair;

They celebrating huge party for us;

We exchanging our wedding rings;

THE END!

The child closes the story book happily;

Yeah!

"The Alluring Fairy Tale", the story ends.

Clouds are rolling;

It is a breezy dusk;

Birds swing their wings towards the nest;

Albert standing in the balcony with guitar;

He gently touches over the strings;

And the strings overwhelmed with sweet music;

Notes flying in the air;

It is rolling, flying and jumping out from the window;

And it visits the bird's nest and they make lullaby to their

chicks;

Then they moving to the valleys, rivers, trees and finally to

the mountain,

And make them to take rest for a while;

Finally, the notes enter into the Teresa's house;

Slowly it gets into her ear and she fall in love with that

music;

That notes melt her heart,

Boost her nerves;

She faints;

Her soul slowly comes out from her body;

All those notes keep her soul safely on the sofa before Albert
eyes;
Albert wakes up Teresa's soul;
But there is no improvement;
Albert confused;
Again, she starts to play the guitar;
The music from his guitar makes her alive with soul and
body;
She is standing in front of him with full of love;
The music connects them apart from so many distances;
Their union will be like,
Strings combining with guitar;
Keys in the keyboard;
Holes in the flute;
Yeah! They are the huge music band;
With this the theater show comes to an end.

A BEAUTIFUL LOVE STORY

The stars are twinkling in the sky;

And the moon dancing behind the clouds;

A ray from the light house trying to touch another end of the

coast;

The waves chasing one and another;

Sound from the sea makes me feel gentle;

Sand from the seashore records our foot prints;

Breezy air just floats like a boat in my skin, I feel light;

Now my body weighs nothing,

Coz our soul wandering in the beach;

Our conversation playing with the air;

Sometimes our giggling sound echoing higher than waves;

Holding your hand and walking for a while make me please;

Now I'm living into your eyes;

Your retina is a zooming lens of my image;

Often your eye lashes clicking snaps;

Your brain is a huge memory card;

It holds thousands of our memory;

I find myself through your eyes;

With this Da Vinci ends his stroke with painting brush;

This is what the entire portrait tries to explain;

A beautiful love story!

A PATH TOWARDS THE TREASURE

There is a huge silence after the heavy rain;

Henna walking through the wet road;

Her path covers with mud puddles;

While walking through the road

She just admires the nature;

She sees,

The water droplets from the leaf slowly reach the puddle;

Oops! Puddle swallows the water drops;

Road side covers with full of trees and green pastures;

Birds are creeping;

Gentle breeze swipes her face now and then;

Her lungs can feel the cool breeze of nature;

Mud puddle reflects her image;

And it looks like the beautiful portrait with sky background;

Sun tries to give yellow shades to the portrait;

Fragrance of the flowers staggers her body;

Often trees shaking their hand;

Oh! They may be the business partners of the nature;

The agents from honey bank collecting interest from the

flowers;

Flies are the best choreographers;

Butterflies painting the world with rainbow;

River holds the treasure;

Henna finds the treasure;

Yup!

She is a fisher woman.

A BROKEN GLOWING TREE

My mind was rolling backwards;

Clocks hands were race with each other,

From dusk to dawn;

I was sinking into the bowl of our memory;

Our last sipped coffee cup was the only vessel in the dining

table;

It had dried after the carnival of ant;

My eyes froze with your last sight;

My entire house plugged with silence;

Emotions play highlighted drama in my house;

And the arrow of your giggling sound punctured my body;

It echoed between four walls;

Resonated with my hearted that tried to defense it,

Your memory was like lightning bolt;

Each second it flashed over me,

I was plumed down like pieces of glass;

My soul tried to rebuild my broken pieces,

Tears glued the grip to it;

All my broken pieces longing for your presence;

My thoughts were deep down in our memory,

My eye balls were slowly rolled towards your direction;

Sudden ray from your retina would set everything straight;

Fallen leaves started to grow;

The whole tree was glowing than before,

Finally, "you were mine and I was your".

NO REASON! WHY?

Her lips utter more than words;

Her eyes express thousands of untold stories;

Her heart obscures millions of memories;

No reason! Why?

Her dark circle on her face accelerates gradually;

Her blood pumps in an exceptional manner;

Her embodiment seems camouflage amidst bones;

No reason! Why?

Her face metamorphoses to blanch;

Her skin stales like barren land;

Her physique is excessively fragile;

No reason! Why?

Her eyes clash with the horrendous flashes of lightning bolts;

Her heart plunge like ashes after the cataclysm;

Her body is gleaming in the eternal flames.

No reason! Why?

SHE!

She was imprisoned in the cage;

Tremendous blocks surrounded her;

She used to enumerate the blocks;

Her limbs were tethered in an apex;

Days were rolling;

She wanted to swing her wings high in the sky;

Prison, only kept opened in the time of food;

Even though it was opened;

She could not fly;

Her restrained shank was wounded;

Gradually it erupted to lacerate her;

She strived to glide,

But fetters dragged her back;

Inchmeal her aspiration stretched strong;

Birds in the next coops advised her to remind there;

They dishearten her;

Her only target was the sky;

She plunked the target;

She shattered the gives and crate;

Said goodbye;

Gave it one's best shot;

And flew high!

QUOTES

"Always strive to be unique.

Your essence should be different from others."

"Don't hold it for too long, if it is so hard;

hold it for life long, if they wait for you too long."

"Do what your heart wants,

go where your mind directs,

and be happy with that, coz nothing wrong in it."

"You may be the king/queen on the chessboard,

I am the only queen for my entire dynasty;

straight forward or checkmate is my choice,

so be careful in your move."

"Being single,

it is a great opportunity to build you.

It shows that you are stronger than others.

And you are the only king/ queen for this entire empire."

"The love is infinity,

when your soul is connected with right one;

the life is extraordinary,

when that love becomes your soul mate."

"Life is like a car journey in national highway;

some may cross your way by mistake or with purpose,

some may overtake to guard you from accidents.

Don't traffic yourself with people and unwanted emotions.

Life is to be happy.

Hold on with moderate gear, switch on rock and roll,

tune up the beat and enjoy your company.

Happy journey readers!!"

"You may lose something while you are walking on the road of

life.

If it is really meant to you, damn! Sure, you will get it back.

If not, you are much more deserved than this."

"Smile, when you are high above;

smile, when you are in deep down;

smile, when your eyes wandering in emotions;

smile, when your heart holds too much;

smile and share your smile;

because, you are the mirror,

so, say cheese to others."

"Life begins with imagination, travels with visualization
and finally ends with realization."

"Life, as sweet as chocolate

as hot as chili,

it's up to you whether you look

forward to the next chocolate

or

staying with that hot chili."

"The world will reject you,

evaluate you,

criticize you,

however, the more you reinforce yourself,

the more brighten you will be in this world."

"100% of happiness starts from 0% of expectation."

"Make yourself as your first priority,

coz no one will do that instead of you."

"No one will understand who you are,

so be proud of being a difficult subject."

"Life is like a mirror of what you show, which only reflects."

"Emotions cannot be hidden under the blanket of the heart."

You can contact the Publisher at:

www.fanatixx.in

or

Call at: +91 8443203204